A LENT COURSE
BASED ON THE MOVIE

RACHEL MANN

DARTON·LONGMAN+TODD
INTELLIGENT • INSPIRATIONAL • INCLUSIVE
SPIRITUAL BOOKS

First published in 2025 by
Darton, Longman and Todd Ltd
Unit 1, The Exchange
6 Scarbrook Road
Croydon CR0 1UH

editorial@darton-longman-todd.co.uk

This product conforms to the requirements of the European
Union's General Product Safety Regulations (GPSR).
EU Authorised Representative for GPSR:
Easy Access System Europe –
Mustamäe tee 50, 10621 Tallinn, Estonia
gpsr.requests@easproject.com

© 2025 Rachel Mann

The right of Rachel Mann to be identified as the Author
of this work has been asserted in accordance with the Copyright,
Designs and Patents Act 1988.

Print book ISBN: 978-1-917362-16-0

No part of this book may be used or reproduced in any
manner for the purpose of training artificial intelligence
technologies or systems.

A catalogue record for this book is available from the British
Library.

Designed and produced by Judy Linard
Printed and bound in India by Replika Press Pvt Ltd

CONTENTS

INTRODUCTION 5

WEEK ONE 'No One Mourns the Wicked' – How do we judge what is good? 15

WEEK TWO 'What is this Feeling?' –Fear and loathing in the land of Oz 35

WEEK THREE 'Dancing Through Life' – What is a life well lived? 53

WEEK FOUR 'Popular' – The attractions and pitfalls of popularity and being liked 71

WEEK FIVE 'Defying Gravity' – The joy and cost of seeing the world clearly and living life authentically 91

POSTSCRIPT 112

INTRODUCTION

One of the many wonderful things about the Christian faith is its invitation to become our truest selves. In Jesus Christ lies a call to discover one's deepest, most flourishing life: to become who you are. I suspect for many outside faith (and indeed for some who have been damaged, chewed up, and spat out by abusive versions of it), my claim will sound either surprising or hollow. Christianity for some – and indeed for me before I came to faith – is a religion which controls and limits rather than sets free. For some who have 'escaped' a stifling Christian upbringing or a vile encounter with one of its authoritarian variants, Christianity is abusive, crushing out individuality, difference, and our longings to live in the truth.

Nonetheless, my own experience runs counter to such accounts. As I have sought, in prayer, love and service, to grow ever more into the likeness of Christ, I have been liberated to be me: 'me' in community and 'me' as a person who does not fit into neat and off-the-shelf categories of being a human or a Christian. In my difference – as an LGBT+ person, as a disabled person, as a neurodiverse person, among other things – I have found a home in Jesus Christ. As much as God challenges me to grow in love, faith, hope and so on, God also delights in my oddness, difference, and strangeness: the embrace of God is an embrace of celebration and joy. Yes, it is costly to follow the path of Christ. It is no pick and mix path and it makes huge demands on us. When I, in my sinfulness, want to close down the field of love, justice, and mercy, God reminds me that his way is not my way. Nonetheless, to follow Christ is to step out on the way to full life.

For those of you who already know the musical *Wicked*, you may begin to see why a Lent book based on part one of its movie adaptation is a less surprising decision than it might otherwise be. For, in the midst of the bright 'major-key' musical numbers – some of which seemingly out-saccharine Disney tunes at their most sweet – and the technicolour blare of Oz, is a story which speaks into deep human desires to be our authentic selves; a longing for authenticity, liberation and to live in the truth of who we are. Not least among the reasons why *Wicked* has become the phenomenon it is, is the way it tells a story of the human desire to break free of constraints which stifle our creative and true selves, and of the inevitable cost that can bring in a society which refuses to respect and nurture difference and honour justice.

While I shall try to keep the focus of this book on part one of the movie adaptation, it is helpful to place it in the wider arc of Stephen Schwartz's musical. It is both a simple childish fable and a clever literary text. While it is possible to watch and enjoy the musical on its own terms, ultimately it is set in the 'universe' of one of the classics of film and literary culture: L. Frank Baum's *The Wizard of Oz*. Schwartz tells an alternative version of the familiar events covered in *The Wizard of Oz*.[1] *Wicked* is both an origin story for key characters in *The Wizard of Oz* as well as a satire on and subversion of the original story/film.

Wicked, then, is what is often call a 'ret-conned' story. 'Ret-conning' is simply the task of giving a new meaning or understanding to a familiar story by writing something that shows it differently. Many of

[1] Schwartz uses Gregory Maguire's 1995 book *Wicked: The Life and Times of the Wicked Witch of the West* as source-material.

Introduction 7

the original ideas in *The Wizard of Oz* are retconned in *Wicked*. At the heart of the retro-fitted Oz story is Elphaba Thropp, a young woman of enormous magical power and – even more importantly – a huge heart for justice and truth, as well as a profound capacity for love; a woman who, because she is different, is scapegoated and used by others; who because she has green skin is the cause of shame for her father. She is blamed for her younger sister Nessa's disability and the death of her mother. *Wicked* is the story of how Elphaba becomes the Wicked Witch of the West, and how the privileged, glamorous Galinda 'Glinda' Upland becomes the Good Witch of the North. The events of *The Wizard of Oz* – the arrival of Dorothy, her wearing of the red jewelled shoes and the downfall of the Wizard – only become part of *Wicked*'s story in its second half, which is the subject of the movie, *Wicked: For Good*. In its overall arc, Schwartz's musical manages a rare thing: to offer a plausible alternative account of the events of *The Wizard of Oz* while revealing that Elphaba and Glinda should not be read simply through the lens provided by the original story.

What lifts *Wicked* above children's fare (great though it can be!) is its handling of profoundly contemporary and timeless themes. The setting may be the magical land of Oz, but at its core *Wicked* is a story for our populist, post-truth times: it exposes and satirises with considerable aplomb the ways in which powerful and privileged people, institutions and governments, can use information to control public narratives. Both Elphaba and Glinda become pawns in the wider political machinations of the fraudulent, but charming Wizard and his lieutenant, Madame Morrible (who is responsible for the hurricane which brings Dorothy to Oz). Behind the glossy 'major key' shininess is a shadier 'minor key' story which suggests that those who have the appearance of good may have dubious, exploitative motives, while those who are represented as ugly and wicked can be the agents of salvation and goodness. It is a classic 'topsy-turvy' or 'upside-down' fable, in which the truth is distorted by perception and propaganda. *Wicked* suggests not only – as the Bible has it – that humans 'see through a mirror dimly,' but that the mirror is so distorted we can barely judge what is true or false, good or evil, hopeful and despairing anymore.

These are big ethical themes. Indeed, *Wicked* has been dismissed by some critics as a simple and simplistic morality tale. I understand why some people feel this diminishes its impact. The criticism is meant to imply that the musical's moral surety impairs its seriousness. I must admit there was a time when – without ever having listened to the music or seen the stage show – I agreed with this critical view. I can be such a snob and the worst kind at that: the sort of snob who does not even make the effort to judge for themselves.

I see things rather differently now. I have seen the stage production fourteen times and part one of the movie version many times in addition. By the time you read this, I shall have seen *For Good* a fair few times too. What I love about *Wicked* is precisely the way in which its silliness and broad humour – brought to life in the movie adaptations by the superb comic timing of Ariana Grande's Glinda – embraces the mythic simplicity of fairy tales and morality plays. By mythic I do not mean 'fake' or 'false' but deep and foundational; myths help us make sense of a puzzling, often bewildering world. It is one of the abiding strengths of the Bible: it is the story of stories which gives us words of life. Yes, the Bible is mythically rich in ways that *Wicked* would not and could not wish to be, yet they share a fascination with our simple longing to make sense of reality. The simplicity of *Wicked* like that of many fairy tales and myths is deceptive; simplicity is not simplistic. Simplicity so often defeats our human gift for over-complication. It challenges the cynical and the sophisticated alike.

This Lent book, then, is an invitation to explore pressing yet perennial human dilemmas and challenges, placing them – ultimately – in the wider frame of the Christian vocation to grow ever more into the likeness of Christ. I want to invite you to do so in a convivial, relaxed and joyous way; thus the focus on such a delightful musical film as *Wicked*. This might strike some as rather counter-intuitive. For, as I have noted in the two previous 'film-based' Lent courses I've written,[2] it is tempting to treat Lent as a time of grim self-denial; as one of the two great Christian seasons of penitence (alongside Advent), the focus of our Lenten discipline is so often shaped around giving up 'bad' and 'indulgent' things (thus the denial of rich foods for example) or taking 'worthy' things on, like a new work of service (volunteering in a food bank), that may feel good, but are costly.

Watching and reflecting on a shiny Hollywood blockbuster, often in convivial company with lots of laughter and joy, hardly seems to fit the classic Lenten profile. Surely, God is not going to be impressed by such an impious approach to Lent? Personally, I think such a view sells God short. I believe that God does not want us to indulge in performative Lenten discipline (especially stuff that looks impressive – 'I've given up this, this and this, you know ... how about you?'). Jesus warns against. Rather, God invites us to go deeper; to attend to what is going on and be faithful to the call of love, mercy, and goodness. This

---

[2] *From Now On* (Darton, Longman and Todd, 2018), based on *The Greatest Showman*, and *Still Standing* (Darton, Longman and Todd, 2020), based on the Elton John biopic, *Rocketman*.

does not need to be a grim task; it is a work of joy. To grow in learning and – even more crucially – in wisdom can be a delight and fun too.

I remain convinced that you cannot keep a good God down and that both the natural world around us as well as our cultural productions – our films, our art and literature, and so on – are shot through with routes to a deeper encounter with the Living God. The world is 'sacramentally charged.' This is not as crude as someone saying, 'oh the narrative arc in that secular story or that secular film is a little bit like Jesus', isn't it?'; rather, I want to suggest that the human themes and narratives embedded and modelled in a film like *Wicked* reflect the truth that we are made in the image of God and called into the likeness of Christ. Our humanity and our divine spark shine through it.

I acknowledge that for some Christians – though, in my experience, very few outside the United States – there may be some controversy about a Lent course based on a musical with witches and wizards at its heart. The Hebrew Bible has notable injunctions against consulting witches. These texts provided theological justification for witchcraft persecutions from the Late Medieval/Early Modern Eras through to the dawn of the Enlightenment. I do not doubt the anxiety felt by some Christians. However, if even fantastical versions of witches and wizards from the world of Oz lead you to worry that watching a movie about them might lead you to stumble into the grip of Satan, this book is not for you. Please move on. My own take on *Wicked* is this: I see no more cause for anxiety about its witches than about its talking animals. To get wound up about them is asinine. There is wickedness in this world, but it is not to be found in this musical; if you want to find wickedness, look to the structural injustice embedded in our economic and political systems as well as our genius for caprice and selfishness. That is worth getting one's knickers in a twist about. If you think *Wicked* is where evil is, or evil enters in, you are looking in the wrong direction.

I hope then that you receive this book with pleasure and openness. It is an invitation to spend time with a delightful, singalong film and dare to look deeper. The stories of Elphaba, Glinda, Fiyero et al are delightful and funny; seemingly as bright and shiny as the land of Oz itself. However, they contain within them fascinating contrasts and suggestive shadows. They hold riches which reward deeper attention, especially in a divided and polarised world such as ours, in which the forces of bigotry and segregation are on the rise and authoritarianism and populism are in danger of becoming the default. *Wicked* deploys fable and fantasy to offer a striking critique and work of resistance to dehumanising and unfair ways of going on. At its heart is a deep longing: for love, friendship and understanding. As the story unfolds we see how readily these virtues can shift into something less attractive: greed, fear, and the love of power. In short, sin. As we enter this season of self-examination and recommitment to the ways of Christ, I trust that this course may offer a fresh way of embracing that call to live flourishing and holy lives.

HOW TO USE THIS BOOK

As with my previous DLT Lent books, *From Now On* and *Still Standing*, I refuse to be overly prescriptive. This is your book. You may use it as you see fit. If, ultimately, you find no value in it, dispose of it. Thank you for at least taking a look. At the same time, I have sought to give serious and considered thought to the structure and content of this course. I hope this attention – borne of a deep love for both the Bible and *Wicked* – means my suggested structure is a reliable guide.

While this is a Lent course designed both to have enough 'give' and enough direction to provide a group with sufficient material to chew on over five sessions, it is also a course that can be used profitably by a person reflecting and praying on their own. Crucially, I have aimed to provide sufficient material that a course leader, or leaders, feel confident to plot their own path through each session. I am sure that some groups, over a period of two hours might gad their way through every section of a session. At the same time, not every group will be able to set aside more than half-an-hour or an hour. I commend, in such circumstances, a permissive approach. Never feel you have to slavishly work your way through every detail, question or even biblical section contained in the course. Please do add alternative biblical passages if you find examples that work better than mine.

Despite (or perhaps because) of my experiences of using Zoom and other digital platforms during the COVID pandemic, I do think it is helpful for groups to meet in person, where possible. It will be important to appropriately accommodate those who feel vulnerable in such a setting, but there is a real dynamic energy in conversation generated when participants are in one room together. At the same time, groups should not feel they have to meet physically in order to study together. There are a lot of online applications out there that can bring people together. Even I, who am frankly something of an analogue person in a digital age, have found value in using different applications to connect with others. It does not, for example, take an enormous amount of skill or perseverance to learn how to share a screen with other participants in, say, a Zoom meeting. This should mean that it is possible

Introduction 13

for someone with a digital version of the film to share a clip with others in an online group.

It should go without saying that, for participants to get the best out of this study guide, it is really helpful for them to have watched the film. For those who wish to study *Wicked* in a group setting, it can be especially helpful for participants to watch the film together. For those of us of a musical turn, it can be tremendous fun to turn that 'watch-party' into a sing-along.[3] It is also worth saying that if the course is being followed in a socially distant manner, and the film is available on a digital platform like Netflix, there are browser apps available to enable people to watch together, simultaneously, and be able to make real time comments. Please note that the timings in the course are based on the digital version. Do double check the timings if you are using Blu-ray or DVD formats.

Wicked is rated 'PG' by the British Board of Film Classification. This means it should be suitable – with parental guidance – for all ages. As such, it is not a controversial film that is likely to trigger trauma reactions. Nonetheless, group leaders should always remember that any film with serious underlying themes regarding stereotyping, othering, bullying and exploitative power like those contained in *Wicked* can generate deep and serious discussion. It is entirely possible that someone might be moved to share something of personal significance that could leave them vulnerable and exposed. Should someone disclose something so personal, it is crucial for group leaders and the wider group to hold those disclosures appropriately. It is worth stating from the outset of each session that a high level of confidentiality will

---

[3] For others, I imagine such an experience would be worthy of one of the lower reaches of Dante's vision of Hell.

be expected within the group setting, as well as the best safeguarding standards expected by the Church.

We owe it to each other to look out for and look after each other. The best way for us to do this is in a context of prayer. Prayer is not simply saying words or keeping silence. It is an intentional relationship between God, us, and each other. It is a way of being in the world. This course is structured through prayer. I offer an opening and closing prayer, but course leaders are welcome to add in other prayer elements as they see fit. Even if you find my prayers unhelpful, I hope no one skips over a short time of prayer at the beginning and end of the session. Some leaders may wish to provide a formal liturgy or quiet time. Group members might wish to lead worship in turn. Those who plan to work with this course individually may wish to weave it into their personal prayer and tradition.

One final note: I am conscious that using a movie for study purposes can exclude those with visual impairment. Do make every effort to include. When I ran film-based courses in a parish, I always used subtitles when showing a film and where possible, added in audio description. Ultimately, however, I do hope that this course is both stimulating and fun. I'm not one of those Christians who think that Lent requires a complete suspension of joy. *Wicked* is not a po-faced film and I hope that as you work through the material in *Gravity Defied* that, in the midst of the deeper journey, there is space for laughter and warmth.

WEEK ONE

'No One Mourns the Wicked'
– How do we judge what is good?

TO START YOU THINKING

I suspect many of us have played a version of the 'Telephone Game'.[4] The game is simple: someone whispers a message in another person's ear. Then the second person tries to repeat it to the next person in the circle. This goes on and on until the message is repeated back to the person who shared it in the first place. Almost inevitably, the message has changed massively as it is passed from ear to ear. The game reminds us how difficult it is for humans to report accurately what we have heard and what has been said. The Telephone Game reveals that we are not very good listeners, unless we train ourselves to be.[5] We hear what we want to hear rather than what is said. Perhaps this reflects our tendency to place ourselves at the centre of our own story; we can find it challenging to attend to what is really going on beyond ourselves.

The Bible provides ample evidence of this self-centredness. Think of Herod Antipas (or, indeed, his predecessor Herod the Great, the monarch responsible for Massacre of the Innocents). Antipas is an example par excellence of the tendency to prioritise self-interest and self-obsession. When he hears reports of Jesus, in his paranoia and cravenness as the person

---

[4] It is also known as 'Chinese Whispers,' though I am unsure whether such a title is appropriate in the modern world.

[5] As a sidebar, I would be intrigued about how this listening game might work among a signing community; provided that players cannot see each others' signing, do signers distort the original message in the way a hearing community does? I suspect the answer is yes.

responsible for John the Baptist's murder, he believes that Jesus is John raised from the dead. Antipas has become consumed by his self-centred actions and is unable to see the big picture of God's good news. The story reminds us that if we are to receive the reports about Jesus as God intends, we must guard against becoming self-centred and consumed with our own bias and agendas. In being called out of ourselves we are invited to see the world as it actually is.

For Christians, the idea of 'good news' is not only a cause for joy but represents the very Word of Life captured in the life, death and resurrection of Jesus Christ. He is the good news, and he commissions his followers to dwell in and to share the good news about him. It is resilient, and its focus on love, mercy, justice and peace is a profound antidote to a world swimming in information, much of it of dubious provenance. Indeed, one of the unavoidable and depressing truths of the social media age is just how difficult it is to distinguish between fake and actual news. Social media sites are open to exploitation by those who wish to generate endless plausible-seeming and readily shareable information. Its genius for untrustworthiness is surely amplified by Artificial Intelligence. Despite AI's 'gift' for hallucinating made-up facts, how long before many of us start to trust its conclusions simply because it presents information in a confident and compelling way?

I find it fascinating that *Wicked* begins with two words: 'Good News', sung by a chorus of ordinary Oz folk. What is this good news of which they sing? Well, the opening of *Wicked* takes place after the denouement of the story; it is a framing device which will enable the story of Elphaba, Glinda et al. to be told in retrospect. The simple Ozians' good news is that Elphaba, the Wicked Witch of the West, 'the wickedest witch there ever was' is dead. The sense of relief in their song is palpable; Elphaba is a figure the Ozians have grown to fear, hate, and blame for all of their society's wrongs.

In the midst of the celebrations Glinda, the beautiful, blonde-haired Good Witch of the North, appears in her Magic Bubble Chariot to confirm the reality of the Good News: 'Let us rejoice, let us be glad …'. I do not mind admitting – as someone who had been raised on the 1939 film, *The Wizard of Oz* – that the first time I saw *Wicked* on stage (with very little foreknowledge of the story) I was in wholehearted agreement with Glinda. For surely, the Wicked Witch of the West, as shown in *The Wizard of Oz*, is one of the most terrifying characters of all time, right up there with the Child Catcher in *Chitty Chitty Bang Bang*. Her death was 'good news' indeed. Of course, we discover as *Wicked* unfolds, that things are not quite the way they seem. Nonetheless, from the very outset, we begin to discern that Glinda is not all she seems and perhaps the 'good news' she touts is not entirely trustworthy. It might even be a 'made-up fact', conveniently deployed for reasons we are yet to comprehend.

Part of the vocation of those who would follow Jesus Christ is to develop the character and wisdom to discern between what is genuinely good news and that which is not. To achieve this level of discrimination (in the best sense of the word) is no easy task, even when one knows that our truest life is found in Jesus Christ. There are and there will always be people who would exploit even the good news of Jesus for wicked and nefarious ends. In a populist era where division is stoked using 'culture war' talking points and dog-whistles, and individuals in authority and with influence often lie with impunity, it can be challenging to sustain a truthful, generous, and compassionate life. While the Bible reveals that God embodies a deeper news, far beyond the understanding of modern media strategies, I am staggered by how often those who confidently call themselves Christians adopt political and social positions which are based in fear and self-interest rather than the Way; the Way which invites us to love our neighbour as ourselves and live for justice, mercy and peace.

PRAYER

O God of Grace and Mercy,
we praise you for the Good News of Jesus Christ
and ask that you illuminate us with your truth
   and love.
In the midst of the many confusions and false messages
of this world grant us wisdom and discernment;
help us to be guided by your grace, mercy and justice
in Jesus Christ, now and for ever.
Amen.

Read
Luke 4:42-44

ICEBREAKER
Wicked begins with a proclamation of 'good news'. What counts as good news for you? Have you ever misheard or mistaken bad news for good news? When was the last time you received some good news and – if you feel able to share it – what was it?

WATCH

From the film's beginning up to the end of the 'No One Mourns the Wicked' sequence (12.05 mins).

The film's beginning is also the epilogue: that is, 'No One Mourns the Wicked' takes place after the denouement of the story. As the film begins, Glinda, the Good Witch of the North and the trusted official spokesperson for the Wizard of Oz, responds to speculation: Elphaba, the Wicked Witch of the West, has (seemingly) died after a girl throws a bucket of water over her. The news begins to spread around Oz, where propaganda posters and warnings about Elphaba are removed from hoardings. Glinda confirms the news in person and invites her fellow Ozians to agree that good will always conquer evil and that truth will outlive lies.

When Glinda is asked about the origin of wickedness, the musical scene shifts to the birth of Elphaba. We learn that Elphaba's father, Frexspar, was the Governor of Munchkinland; his relationship with his wife, Melena, is fraught, and a charming stranger, a travelling salesman, has an affair with her, fired up by a mysterious green elixir. Melena falls pregnant and Frexspar is delighted until the baby is born. She is green and he is disgusted and horrified.

This rejection is amplified by her impulsive telekinetic powers. We see Elphaba and her disabled sister Nessa as children, talking about the wonderful Wizard of Oz. We also see how Elphaba is mocked by the village children for being different. She attacks them. We begin to sense that she wants to meet the Wizard who can grant her her heart's desire: to be 'normal'. As we return to the present, Glinda reminds the gathered crowd that 'it couldn't have been easy' for Elphaba with a childhood like that. Nonetheless, the chorus takes up its refrain that Elphaba's death is good news and there is joy throughout the land as the image of Elphaba burns.

Think about
Can you think of examples from real life where people have been duped into mistaking falsehood or 'fake news' for reality? What strategies do you use to resist propaganda or trickery? Have you ever fallen for lies and, if so, how did that make you feel?

Glinda raises the question about whether wickedness or evil is something that some people are born with ('innate') or whether it is the product of experience or our environment. What do you think and why?

Glinda also suggests that 'the wicked die alone' and nothing grows for them. To what extent do you think this is a comforting fantasy in an unfair world or is there truth to her claim?

GOING DEEPER

Read
John 7:1-24

In this excerpt from John's gospel, Jesus is in the Temple for the Feast of Tabernacles or Sukkot. In biblical times, it was a feast of pilgrimage in which the faithful were expected to travel to Jerusalem. It is a token of Jesus' faithfulness that this scene unfolds in the Temple (though he initially goes to Jerusalem in secret for he is aware that the authorities are out to get him). More broadly, Sukkot is and remains a harvest festival and to this day observant Jews build temporary booths or tabernacles, in memory of the temporary structures Jewish farmers would have used in antiquity during the harvest season. It is also a festival of hospitality and openness; in addition to welcoming friends and family, on each of the seven days of the festival, an ancestral guest is welcomed, including Abraham, Isaac, Jacob, Moses and David.

Jesus enters the Temple half-way through the Festival and begins to teach. He is aware that he is perceived as a threat; even among those who follow him there are people who do not trust him. In the midst of a festival which celebrates God's blessing and munificence, Jesus exposes the extent to which even God's Word is open to rejection. Jesus Christ, the Son of God, is not seen for who he is; he is greeted with suspicion. Some say he is demon-possessed; others are stunned by his teaching. The crowd cannot yet make up its mind about the Very Love of God drawn close to them; they judge by mere appearances rather than judging correctly.

It is often said, 'Do not judge a book by its cover.' Yet, both Elphaba and Jesus are rejected on the basis of appearances. Why do you think humans draw quick judgments about others based on flimsy evidence?

Jesus suggests that to live well requires exercising 'correct' or 'good' judgment. What are the virtues and skills we can cultivate or deploy in order for us to make 'correct judgments'?

In this passage, Jesus seems to make tough judgments against the people of God, in part because they rely on appearances rather than reality. What, in your view, are the superficial things Jesus judges the contemporary church for?

WATCH

From the end of 'No One Mourns the Wicked' (12.05 mins) to the point where Glinda is carried off (25.55 mins).

As 'No One Mourns ...' ends, one of the Ozians asks Glinda if the rumour that she was once friends with Elphaba is true. Initially, to the shock of the crowd, she says 'Yes'. She then qualifies this by saying their paths crossed, though we, the audience, get to see Glinda's inner thoughts: that she and Elphaba were much closer than that. We discover that Glinda and Elphaba met at Shiz University, when the former was known as 'Galinda.' This leads into a flashback to their first day at college. Galinda arrives in great state, the perfect princess, immediately fawned upon by sycophantic students. Elphaba arrives and frightens the student body. Galinda uses condescending pity to show her 'concern' for Elphaba and reveals she plans to study sorcery and one day could help Elphaba to lose her greenness.

We discover that Elphaba is not at Shiz to study, but is there under the instructions of her father to support her wheelchair-using younger sister, Nessa. We are introduced to Madame Morrible the Dean of Sorcery Studies who is greeted rapturously. Galinda approaches Madame Morrible about studying sorcery. Madame Morrible says she only teaches when there is talent and walks off. The Head Shizstress, Miss

Coddle, decides to help Nessa, against her will, and when Elphaba tries to stop her, she provides a display of wild, undisciplined natural magical skills which grabs the attention of Madame Morrible. Morrible pretends that she is responsible but offers to teach Elphaba. By mistake, Galinda 'volunteers' to room with Elphaba.

Think about
Stereotyping and mockery remain all too common. In our own society who is likely to be the target of such behaviour? What can be the impact of such mockery and stereotyping?

How does Elphaba initially respond to Galinda and the other students' reaction to her? Why, in your view, does she use this strategy?

To what extent does Galinda's speech about one day 'healing' Elphaba of her skin 'issue' have echoes of Christians praying for God to heal disabled people? Does Galinda and other students' responses to Elphaba have echoes of racism in our own society?

Many say, 'Schooldays are the best days of our lives.' However, many of us have mixed memories of school, college, or university. What were some of the best aspects of being in education? If you feel confident to talk about it, what were some of the worst?

GOING DEEPER

Read
Luke 10:25-37

The Parable of the Good Samaritan is so famous it has become part of the cultural fabric. There is no need to be a person of faith to know its outlines. Jesus tells it as part of a conversation with a student of the Torah, the Jewish Law; a person passionate, then, about what God might be saying to his people and keen to fulfil the gift that is the Law. The conversation begins with an exchange about inheriting eternal life and Jesus affirms the lawyer for his excellent summary of the nature of the Law: Love God with your whole heart, mind, body and soul and love your neighbour as yourself. The parable emerges however when the Lawyer wants to know exactly to whom the notion of 'neighbour' refers. Jesus gives a startling answer: the one who shows mercy, even if they are outside the community of family, friends and acceptable social relationships.

In Jesus' world, the Samaritans claimed a common ancestor with the Jews; in very many ways, they were closely connected together with shared scriptures and a belief in one God, yet they were deeply divided from one another. To what extent to do you think divisions and mistrust are most readily generated by people who are most like one another?

In both the world of Oz and our own society, people are so often divided into insiders and outsiders, in-groups and out-groups. To what extent does the idea of 'neighbour' help us to break down such divisions?

The Samaritan in the parable is – unlike the priest and the Levite – an outsider. The parable's first audience would not have expected him or her to stop for a Jew in bandit country. Prejudice and bias get in the way of the audience seeing the Samaritan with respect. Perhaps the same applies to Elphaba as she arrives at university. What can we do to subvert our instincts to privilege people 'more like us'?

WATCH

From 25.55 mins to the end of 'The Wizard and I' (32.18 mins).

After Elphaba's extraordinary display of power, Madame Morrible talks to her about her 'talent'; initially, Elphaba cannot see her power as anything other than destructive, but Morrible explains that it is possible to control these gifts and if she can she will get to meet the Wizard and perhaps even become his 'Magical Grand Vizier'.

Elphaba becomes excited about meeting her idol, the Wizard. We learn more about her deepest desires: not only her longing for recognition from the Wizard, but her hope that she will find in him someone who will see her for who she really is. If she can gain his approval, she thinks that no one will think she is strange. Finally, she reveals her deepest desire: that the Wizard will ultimately 'degreenify' her. Accompanying this hope, she has a vision of the future in which she will be the cause of a 'celebration throughout Oz'.

Think about
Elphaba has a powerful need for affirmation, recognition and for a place of honour. How understandable do you find this desire given what we know about her? Or do you think it reveals a moral or personal weakness she needs to address?

At one point, Elphaba sings, 'Shouldn't a girl who's so good inside have a matching exterior?' What do you make of this statement?

Can you see any connections between Elphaba's desire to be 'degreenified' and the impact of racism and colonialism in a world which tends to privilege 'whiteness' over other skin colours?

GOING DEEPER

Read
2 Corinthians 4:5-18

St Paul's Second Letter to the Corinthians is a moving and personal epistle in which Paul reveals his vulnerability. In it he responds to criticism about his style and approach to leadership and, most particularly, his work as an apostle. He writes some of his most moving and striking lines, revealing his inner life in a way that is rare in ancient writings.

In chapter four, Paul reminds the young church in Corinth that his work is not to proclaim himself, but Jesus Christ as Lord. Paul reminds us and himself that we have the 'treasure' of heaven in 'clay jars' so that we know that the truth belongs to God and does not come from us. Here, is a profound echo of Jeremiah's deep wisdom that in the hands of God we are like clay in the potter's hand; how readily we crack, break, and fail. In a classic piece of Pauline rhetoric, he tells the Corinthians that he is afflicted in every way, but not crushed. He is struck down but not destroyed, always carrying within his body the death of Jesus so that Jesus' life might also be visible. He holds death within himself so that the Corinthians may have life within themselves.

Paul does not lose heart or faith despite his limitations or persecutions. He holds onto the deep knowledge that the one who raised the Lord Jesus will raise us also and bring us with Jesus into God's presence. He encourages the Corinthians to take heart by trusting not in the superficial but in the inner, deeper hope of the Good News. He says, 'even though our outer nature is wasting away, our inner nature is being renewed day by day'. He looks not at what can be seen but at what cannot be seen, for what can be seen is temporary, but what cannot be seen is eternal.

In the film *Chariots of Fire*, the Christian Olympic Gold Medal winner and evangelist, Eric Liddell, famously says – after Paul – 'Where does the strength to run the race come from? From within.' How important is inner strength and the inner life?

Elphaba seems to want both recognition of her inner life but also to have what can be seen – her skin colour – changed. How does this sit alongside what Paul says in 2 Corinthians? (On the other hand, in a biased and prejudiced society which privileges one skin colour over another, might it be argued that cherishing what is seen really matters?)

Paul and Elphaba each make themselves vulnerable. What are the similarities and differences between what they say/sing?

LOOKING AHEAD ... ACTIVITIES TO CONSIDER THIS WEEK

Hopefully, this week's session has given you some resources through which to reflect on the gaps between how we see ourselves (and others see us) and how God beholds us in our fullest selves. We are reminded that we are limited creatures who are marked not only by our wounds, scars and doubts, but that we are also the beloved of God. We are made in the image of God and called to grow into the likeness of Christ. In my experience, that work of growth is a lifetime's work. Nonetheless, that growth is real when we attend to Jesus. The way we do that is in prayer and worship and by seeking to be obedient to his Way. So much of life is about cultivating good habits. This applies as much in prayer and holy action as it might with diet and exercise.

So, this week, take an opportunity to recommit yourself to God in Jesus Christ by paying close attention in prayer and action to that which builds up the community in love and grace. Perhaps pray for a clearer, kinder understanding of yourself and others, asking God to remind you not only that he loves you, but that he likes you. Perhaps pray for an enemy or someone you struggle with. Consider what actions you might take this week to build up your community – church or local community. Can you donate time and/or money to an anti-bullying programme or community cohesion group?

This week's closing prayer was composed by Richard of Chichester and made famous when used in the song 'Day by Day' from Stephen Schwartz's 1970 musical *Godspell*. It may well be a good framing prayer for your daily devotions this coming week as well.

CLOSING PRAYER
Thanks be to thee, my Lord Jesus Christ,
for all the benefits thou hast given me,
for all the pains and insults thou hast borne for me.
O most merciful redeemer, friend and brother,
may I know thee more clearly,
love thee more dearly,
and follow thee more nearly, day by day.
Amen.

REFLECTIONS

Use this space to record thoughts, responses and resolutions that have occurred to you during Week One.

WEEK TWO

**'What is this Feeling?' –
Fear and loathing in the land of Oz**

TO START YOU THINKING

I wonder if there are things which – years after the fact – continue to haunt you. I am not talking about ghosts or spectres, or the hauntings we might see featured in a sensationalist documentary, or a popular podcast series like *Uncanny*. I mean things you have done which, for years and years, you cannot quite let go (or they will not let you go) because you feel guilt, shame, or embarrassment. For example, I am now in my mid-fifties, but I am still, quietly, and unaccountably, haunted by something I did when I was seventeen.

When I was seventeen, I was a bully, along with half-a-dozen other so-called 'cool' or 'popular' kids in my Sixth Form. Like so much bullying it began as a joke; while I was not the person who kicked off the 'joke' I used my insecure need for popularity and attention to bolster my status. It is no justification (there can be none), but close friends and I didn't recognise what we were doing as bullying because it did not fit our picture of bullying: after all, we were not stealing a vulnerable kid's money or valuables or beating him or her up. This was middle-class, 'white collar' bullying: psychological, readily hidden, based on innuendo and word play.

Essentially, my friends and I started bullying a vulnerable young woman because she was different. She did not fit our idea of feminine beauty or deportment; she dressed like she was much older than she was. She was a committed conservative

Christian, and this made her an oddity. The bullying began as name calling – I shall not repeat the name we used. It was, in and of itself, innocuous. It was no slur word. But it was cruel when applied to her. We 'insiders' thought it oh so funny. Then that wasn't enough. Some of us started doing impersonations of the children's TV character whose name we had given her. Then a game emerged in which we tried to do these impersonations or use the name in her presence, but – we thought ourselves so clever – in a way we thought she could not spot. It was pathetic and childish and, ultimately, it was devastating. For, of course, our target, our victim, knew that we were being horrible to her and she felt paralysed and lost and isolated. In the end, she had a complete breakdown and left the school.

Why am I telling you this? Not as self-justification or to gain any sympathy. I deserve none. As it happens, the woman who we targeted made a full recovery from our abuse and, indeed, ultimately, I and some others met with her to talk things through. To ask forgiveness and begin to make amends. She forgave us. She had moved on. That doesn't make this teenaged bullying okay. Far from it. The reason I am telling you about this is to remind us how readily we can slip into wicked, abusive ways. Our longings to belong or be part of the inside or powerful group can readily translate into bullying and abuse. I also want to remind us that things that look innocuous can become extraordinarily toxic very rapidly and the ripples and echoes of bullying can travel across decades. I cannot speak for the survivor, but I know I have never been the same. I try to stand up against bullying in its countless forms when I see it. While school and university might be prime times for the dynamics of in-groups and cliques to play out, frankly such behaviour can and does happen everywhere: at work, at sports clubs and in church. None of us is immune from it, whether we have faith or none. Faith communities can be the worst.

For the non-religious, there can be real shock in discovering that bullying and power-games apply as much in church and religious settings as the secular world. There can be a belief that church people are better than others; holier, somehow. Otherwise, what is the point of the Church, if it makes its adherents no different from the rest of the world? I do understand this. That is how I felt before I became a Christian. Now, I understand that the church does not exist for the holy and righteous but for those who are only too aware of how far they are falling short of God's love. The Church is about failing people seeking God together.

Nonetheless, what I struggle with is the Church's serial inability to address power imbalances and bullying and deference. Time and again, the Church – of which I am a part – has excused and indeed promoted those who bully, charm, and exploit. The words of Jesus at the Sermon on the Mount – blessed are the poor, blessed are those who mourn and so on – are so readily ignored. The Church has so very far to go and so often it feels almost impossible to stay within it. Jesus Christ cries out with the victims of exploitation, bullying and abuse and he waits for you, me and all of us to attend. And sometimes we do. And I am convinced that God will not bless and hallow the Church unless we do and then act on it.

For all that *Wicked* is perfect singalong material, I sense that one reason for its popularity is the way it captures the rivalries, in-groups and out-groups and insecurities of youth. In the dynamics between Galinda and Elphaba it exposes the readiness with which we can become bullies and abusers and thereby mistreat others. Part of the reason a story like *Wicked* has grip is because it reflects real life rivalries, insecurities, and needs. However, for all that our teenage and younger years may be marked by an amplified desire for belonging and to be part of a group, it is not limited to that part of life. To be in the company of those we perceive to be glamorous or powerful or just to be with those whom we see as 'like us' can be ravishing.

PRAYER

O God of Justice and Mercy,
we come before you as frail and limited flesh
longing to grow into your likeness and promise;
grant us grace to attend to you
and be shaped by your love, peace and hope.
Help us to be a community of justice and truth
resisting all that breaks down and impairs
the flourishing of life in all its fulness.
May we have courage to face the sins of the Church
and of ourselves and act for all that is right,
in Jesus Christ our Lord.
Amen.

Read
Matthew 25:31-36

Icebreaker
(As ever, please only share insofar as you feel safe or it is appropriate to do so.) Have you ever been part of a clique or in-group? How did it feel? Or have you experienced being on the outside looking in? As Christians, what kind of behaviour should we seek to embody?

WATCH

From Elphaba walking down a corridor to her dorm (32:19 mins) up to the end of 'What Is This Feeling?' (39:01 mins).

In this scene, we witness the first proper encounter between Galinda and Elphaba, the new room-mates. Elphaba discovers that Galinda has taken over the entire dorm, apart from one dusty corner. Galinda has possessions galore and says, 'the rest of my stuff will arrive shortly'. Galinda tries to persuade Elphaba to get her into Madame Morrible's sorcery class, leading to an uncontrolled explosion of Elphaba's powers. The scene then moves to each woman writing a letter to their parents, as they try to describe their roomie. It becomes clear that Elphaba and Galinda cannot bear each other. Equally, the entire University thinks Galinda walks on water and is completely the wronged party; Elphaba stands alone but apparently also refuses to be intimidated and takes pleasure in scaring Galinda.

Think about
To what extent do you think Galinda and Elphaba have legitimate reasons for loathing one another? Why do you think Galinda has the support of the student body?

What do you think about Elphaba's strategy for dealing with the university-wide negativity towards her?

Have you ever loathed someone completely, whether out of jealousy or envy? What did that feel like? Has this dislike ever worked through into a friendship?

The priest James Martin SJ has written about the power of envy. He tells a story about how, when he was a novice, he was envious of a fellow novice's devotion in prayer. At the end of the year, he spoke to this colleague saying he wished he could be like him; his colleague replied that he had spent all year envying Martin's commitment to social justice. Does this suggest that envy is the product of our inability to accept ourselves for what we are?

GOING DEEPER

Read
Matthew 5:43-48

Jesus never ceases to amaze, disturb and shock me. This justly famous passage from Matthew is a classic example of why. He subverts our instinct to love those who are closest to us. Rather, Jesus says, to those who would follow him, 'Love your enemies and pray for those who persecute you.' This is no mere moral advice. This is the path for those who wish to become children of the Living God. Jesus reminds us that God the Father sends sun and rain on the evil and the good, the righteous and on the unrighteous alike.

The passage concludes with a series of questions or challenges for us to consider: if you love those who love you, what reward do you have? Do not even those lacking righteousness (he gives the example of tax collectors) do that? And if you greet only your brothers and sisters, what more are you doing than others? He reminds those of us who would follow him that to love only those whom we know and care about is something that those outside the community of faith do. So what makes us distinctive? He concludes: Be perfect, therefore, as your heavenly Father is perfect.

When you read this passage what is your first reaction to it?

What would Elphaba and Galinda's nascent relationship look like if they applied Jesus' words?

Jesus tells us to 'be perfect'. What do you understand by that phrase? Galinda is treated as perfect by her sycophantic friends. How might Jesus view her?

WATCH

From students crossing the quad (39.06 mins) to the end of Dr Dillamond's conversation with Elphaba (43.55 mins) and then from Dr Dillamond leaving to go home (46.25 mins) up to the end of 'Something Bad' (50.06 mins).

In the first clip, we meet Dr Dillamond, the history professor. We discover that he cannot say Galinda and calls her Glinda. Galinda and her clique become increasingly annoyed with him and laugh at him. Galinda's irritation becomes another spark for a verbal tussle between her and Elphaba, who defends Dr Dillamond by saying, 'Some of us are just different.' Dr Dillamond then gives a short lecture on why there are now so few animals teaching at Shiz University. He explains that once there were many animals who taught, but that has become rare. Animal culture has been rejected.

He suggests that the shift in the respect and goodwill towards animals was caused by the Great Drought. Food grew scarce and, according to the Doctor, when this happens people begin to look for someone to blame. He reminds the class that it is impossible to escape the past and we ignore it at our peril. When he attempts to share a timeline to help clarify this statement, the blackboard reveals that someone has replaced it with a handwritten message: 'Animals should be seen and not heard.' Everyone is shocked. Dr Dillamond is angry and asks who is responsible for the message. When no answer is given, the class is dismissed. Elphaba stays behind to support and comfort him; they become friends, in solidarity with one another in their difference and outsider status.

In the second clip, Elphaba follows Dr Dillamond home and eavesdrops on a secret meeting between him and a group of other animals. Dr Dillamond speaks about how animals are being silenced and blamed for everything. He suspects something huge is happening in Oz, targeting animal culture: some animals who speak out are disappearing/being disappeared or losing their jobs. Animals are losing their power to speak at all. Elphaba has a flashback to being treated as lesser herself and has a vision of a caged Dr Dillamond. He explains that 'If you make it discouraging enough, you can keep anyone silent.' Elphaba says that someone needs to speak to the Wizard about this awful situation. Dr Dillamond wants her to keep silent, but Elphaba says the reasons we have a Wizard is to stop bad things happening. As they sing together, Dr Dillamond suddenly and disturbingly begins to bleat rather than speak.

Think about
What, if any, are the parallels between the scapegoating of the animals in Oz and situations in our own world? What are the factors that stoke fear and hatred in our world?

Dr Dillamond suggests it is impossible to escape the past and we ignore it at our peril. How do you respond to that claim?

Elphaba displays solidarity with Dr Dillamond. Why? Does a shared experience of being different always lead to solidarity or not?

What do you make of Dr Dillamond's claim that

'if you make it discouraging enough you can keep anyone silent'? What are the factors which can silence someone or a group of people? Why can it be so challenging to speak up, and for whom are we called to speak up in our society?

GOING DEEPER

Read
Philippians 4:4-14

I return to Paul's Letter to the Philippians when I need to be lifted, inspired, and filled up with hope. It is a work of affection, humility and deep truth. In our excerpt, taken from Paul's closing remarks, he exhorts the Church at Philippi to rejoice and show forth gentleness. In the midst of his own suffering and trials he reminds them not to worry but make prayer with thanksgiving. When they do that, God's peace will guard their hearts and minds in Christ Jesus.

Paul expresses his own rejoicing at the care the Philippians have shown to him, even though they are physically separated from one another. He says, most beautifully and helpfully, that though he suffers, nonetheless he is content with whatever he has. He has seen plenty and lack; he has known the good times and the bad and still he remains generous and content. For truly he knows where abundance lies: in Christ Jesus.

Sometimes people behave selfishly and fearfully when they think there is not enough to go around. Paul's trust in God's provision and abundance is both challenging and comforting. How do you respond?

Dr Dillamond speaks of how famine (and by implication other disasters, natural or human-made) can lead people to want a scapegoat/someone to blame. How might seeking to dwell in a trust in God's abundance offer a powerful counter and resistance to such scapegoating?

In situations where we might feel silenced, persecuted or marginalised, can being people of thanksgiving and rejoicing offer a powerful response? Why?

LOOKING AHEAD ... ACTIVITIES TO CONSIDER THIS WEEK

We live in an inequitable society. The gap between the 'haves' and the 'have-nots' has only widened since the 1970s. There are more billionaires now than at any other time in history, yet food bank use has also skyrocketed. Those who have much often only seem to want more and the attitude of many is that resources are so scarce that there is not enough to go around.

Nonetheless, as people of faith, we are called to embrace a biblical vision of abundance: God provides a world of abundance and all that is needed for the people to thrive and live well. God invites us to cultivate thankfulness in response. Crucially, I do not think this is an apology for the status quo, in which no political questions are asked, and unjust, inequitable situations cannot be challenged. Rather, by cultivating thankfulness, we ourselves are changed. As we recognise God's abundant generosity, we discover that we are called into generosity: of spirit, of sharing of self and of resources. We become less defended and suspicious. I often wonder what the world would look like if the spiritual discipline of thankfulness were practised en masse. I suspect it might look rather different.

Perhaps it is better to start small. So, this week, in your prayer and action, seek to cultivate thankfulness. Look for the glimmer of grace and say thank you to God for it. Give thanks for the big things and the small things and the surprising things. Once we start to look, the field of thankfulness tends to grow. And, as we do this, let us link this thankfulness to generosity. Whether we are materially rich or poor or spiritually rich or poor, there is always space for more generosity. Why? Because there is always more God to be known and embraced. God gives and gives and though we are not God, in growing into his likeness I am confident that the poverty of my own actions can show forth ever greater riches.

CLOSING PRAYER

Generous and abundant God,
thank you for life and love and promise;
thank you for this day and this moment
and this breath. Help us to be alert
to the breaking in of your Kingdom
in this needful and troublous world;
grant us an ever-deeper joy in serving you
as we seek to follow the Way of your son
our saviour Jesus Christ.
Amen.

REFLECTIONS

Use this space to record thoughts, responses and resolutions that have occurred to you during Week Two.

WEEK THREE

'Dancing Through Life' –
What is a life well lived?

TO START YOU THINKING

I have never been much of a dancer. I have shuffled my way through 'last dances' at school discos, head-banged and moshed at heavy metal gigs, become part of the loved-up masses at nightclubs, and – once – I tried and really enjoyed line dancing. I guess you might say – in the midst of my inept grasp of movement and dance – that the most I can hope for is to dance like no one is watching.

The title of this week's session is taken from the song which introduces the privileged, handsome, and feckless Prince Fiyero Tigelaar. He has lived a life of ease and comfort; he has 'danced through life' with barely a care and, repeatedly, has been thrown out of various schools with few if any consequences. He is lazy and self-indulgent yet always lands on his feet. He is idolised by those around him. The ordinary rules of conduct do not apply. In our world, he is like a high-profile celebrity, a billionaire, and royalty all wrapped up into one. His life is practically frictionless and the things for which the rest of us might be censured or even prosecuted simply glance off him. He suggests that the kind of reckless, feckless, and unexamined life he leads is the best life; he encourages the rest of the student cohort to join him in his dance through life.

Can we even begin to suggest that an 'unexamined' life, led simply for pleasure and self-indulgence, is ever a life well lived? The film surely does not. However, when I was teenager, I suspect a huge part of me would have said yes. All I wanted was to be given lots of money, space and opportunity to mess around! One does not need to be young to take such an approach. If there is no deeper value or significance to life or if the planet is doomed, why not choose a life of pleasure if you have the means to do so? I have sometimes been told to live my best life. So often that seems to resolve down to an invitation to 'dance through life' in an individualistic and self-indulgent way.

There are other pictures of dancing, some of which remind us of our vocation to be those who follow the way of Jesus Christ. A few years ago, a friend who loves and teaches country dancing gave me a most liberating theological insight into the beauty and power of dance. She and her husband run dances using John Playford's seventeenth-century *The English Dancing Master* as their guide. These dances gained enormous popularity in the eighteenth century and form the backbone of those found in the original novels (and adaptations) of Jane Austen. By turn lively, stately, formal and fun, they are the kind of dances which, in Austen's rule-bound society, offered young middle-class people the best chance of meeting and conversing, touching and courting. The crucial thing I learned from my friend was that they require co-operation and place the individual in the hands of others. Each partner has to wait on and trust not only their consort but their fellow dancers too.

You may feel it is a little too obvious to say that dancing with a partner or partners is a co-operative matter. I still think it is worth pointing out. We live in a culture where 'doing my own thing' is often seen not only as good but as the norm. Certainly, we need people who are prepared to 'dance' alone, metaphorically if not literally: such pioneers can surprise us and show us new things.[6] However, the richest, most extraordinary dances are dependent on working with established

---

[6] This is a point worth returning to in the final week of this course, when Elphaba decides to 'defy gravity'.

forms and require a honed intimacy and trust. They require relationship.

Some theologians have suggested that the relationship between the Trinity – Father, Son and Spirit – is a kind of divine dance. Their dance is grounded in intimacy, trust, and relationship. It has waiting and tenderness and co-operation inscribed in it; it builds up and together rather than being about self-indulgence and showing off. It is generative too: something new and fresh emerges as the dance unfolds. It is not, then, simply the repetition of old forms or boring conventions. It is a model of how we are invited to live our pilgrimage through this bewildering world. Even if we are called to 'dance through life', the divine vision offers a much richer picture than the self-centred, selfish approach commended by the Fiyeros of this world.

OPENING PRAYER

O Holy God, Blessèd Trinity,
we praise you for your dance of love
which sets the world alight
with your mercy, grace and hope.
As we seek to dwell in you, form us
into your likeness. Help us to unite
our wills and actions to the Way of Jesus Christ,
save us from selfishness and self-absorption
and as we sing your song, teach us the steps
which lead to salvation, now and for ever.
Amen.

Read
Psalm 139:1-6 and 23-24

Icebreaker
Who are the people who inspire you? What is it about their approach to life which inspires you and reveal a life well lived?

LEADERS' NOTE*: This session focuses on the extended 'Dancing Through Life' sequence, which introduces Prince Fiyero and takes the students to the Ozdust Ballroom. Please be prepared to stop the film in the middle of the song 'Dancing Through Life'.*

WATCH

From Elphaba walking away from Dr Dillamond's meeting, through the woods and 'bumping into' Fiyero (50.10 mins) to the point in *Dancing Through Life* where Boq asks Nessa to come with him to the Ozdust Ballroom (60.52 mins).

In this section of the sequence, we meet the charming and handsome Prince Fiyero who has transferred to Shiz from the Royal Winkie Academy. He almost crashes into Elphaba on his horse and there is an immediate spark between them. Fiyero is shocked to discover that she is the first girl not to be immediately bowled over by him.

Galinda hears of Fiyero's arrival and immediately sets out to win his heart, dressing up and using all the allure she has to get his attention. Meanwhile Fiyero charms everyone, apart from Elphaba. He shares his philosophy of life – to dance through life, never trying because those who don't try never look foolish. He invites every student to try the 'unexamined life'. Galinda and Fiyero flirt and he asks if she ever goes to the Ozdust Ballroom. It is off-limits, as the munchkin Boq points out. However, Fiyero's charm and glamour is such that no one except Elphaba can resist breaking the rules to go with him, least of all, Galinda. As the school readies itself to follow Fiyero, Boq reveals his love for Galinda. Galinda uses this devotion to deflect him away, convincing him to show his devotion by inviting Nessa to the Ozdust. Nessa is thrilled to be invited.

Think about
Fiyero is charming, wealthy, and glamorous. What is it about those qualities that we find so attractive or compelling? (Or do you disagree with that claim? If so, why?) Have you ever fallen for or been compromised by people using their charm, wealth or glamour to get their own way?

The philosopher Socrates famously claimed, 'the unexamined life is not worth living.' Fiyero turns this upside down and suggests that a life of pleasure and self-indulgence is a better way to live. What do you think? Can you see the attractions of Fiyero's approach?

What do you make of the emerging dynamic between Fiyero and Galinda as well as between Fiyero and Elphaba?

What do you think of Galinda using Boq, whose name she cannot be bothered to say correctly, to invite Nessa to the Ozdust Ballroom?

GOING DEEPER

Read
Matthew 13:1-9

I sometimes wonder what Jesus' original audience made of the parable of the sower and the seed. Were they blown away? Puzzled? Nonplussed? Would you think me a terrible Christian if I said that I find it a bit boring? It is such a famous parable that it is difficult to consider it fresh or – dare I say it – even terribly interesting.[7]

[7] I surely cannot be alone in not getting terribly excited about preaching on this parable.

Perhaps its power is undercut by knowing Jesus' own explication of it. However, what if we were to read it as a cautionary tale about living a shallow, unexamined life? In this version, 'seeds' which promise deeper self-knowledge sometimes fall on a path where there is no opportunity for them to grow and they are gobbled up; other seeds fall on rocky ground with little soil and though there is seemingly rapid growth in self-knowledge there is no true depth and the lack of roots means the growth withers away. Others lose their way with the cares of the world, while some seeds of promise fall on those who are truly receptive and this produces wisdom.

Assuming there is mileage in this reading of the parable, what are its implications for how we might seek to live our lives?

Does the parable of the Sower imply that being fruitful or having wisdom or faith is a matter of chance?

What can we do not to be like a stony path or rocky ground or be caught up in the cares of the world?

Who, if anyone in *Wicked*, seems most likely to offer the fertile ground for the growth of wisdom? Why do you think that?

WATCH

From Boq and Nessa's conversation (60.52 mins) up to the end of 'Dancing Through Life', when Elphaba and Galinda run off into the night (1hr 16.40 mins).

As Boq speaks to Nessa, Fiyero acknowledges Galinda's manipulative skills. They flirt and tell each other that they are perfect and deserve to be together. Nessa tells Elphaba that Boq has asked her out and explains that it was Galinda who encouraged him to do so. Nessa interprets this positively and warns Elphaba not to say anything against Galinda. Elphaba begins to wonder if Galinda is not so bad after all. Meanwhile, as Galinda prepares for the Ozdust Ballroom, her clique finds a 'horrible' black hat. Galinda decides to give it to Elphaba, pretending it is cool, when really it is a token of how much she dislikes her.

Elphaba is taken in by the ruse, believing that the hat is a sign that Galinda is good; as a quid pro quo, she decides to speak to Madame Morrible about Galinda joining the sorcery seminar. When the class goes to the Ozdust Ballroom, Boq tries to confess to Nessa the reason why he invited her, but cannot bring himself to tell the truth when it is clear that she thinks it is because he pitied her.

Before Elphaba arrives, Madame Morrible appears and gives Galinda a 'training wand' and says she can join the sorcery seminar. The reason? Elphaba will leave it if she doesn't allow Galinda to join. Galinda begins to realise the consequences of her mean actions and wants to stop Elphaba from arriving at the Ozdust in the horrible hat. Elphaba arrives and is greeted by near universal mockery and derision. Even her own sister, Nessa, recoils in embarrassment. Galinda is clearly beginning to feel remorse.

Elphaba decides to dance alone despite the mockery. Fiyero is in awe saying she does not care what others think. Galinda is more insightful and says that of course she does. She makes the decision to start dancing with Elphaba despite this laying her open to mockery herself. Her clique tries to stop her. As Galinda begins to mimic Elphaba's dance, there is a slow thawing of their relationship, until they are dancing as one. Elphaba cries as everyone joins them. The two women hug and then run off into the night as friends.

Think about
Galinda's behaviour is judged consistently to be good, despite her manipulation and selfishness. Why in your view do some people seem to live 'charmed lives'?

To what extent is Galinda's shift in behaviour towards Elphaba (after she receives Madame Morrible's news) a sign of a stirring conscience. Or is it still driven by self-interest? Or is it more complex than that?

How do you respond to Elphaba's solo, silent dancing? This scene also reveals how much Elphaba is carrying, emotionally and psychologically; we see just how awesomely lonely she is and how much she longs for connection and love. How do you respond to this?

GOING DEEPER

Read
John 8:25-38

'The truth will set you free.' These are some of Jesus' most quoted and potent words (though in some translations he says, 'The truth will make you free'). In my own life – as I have negotiated the realities of a disabled and chronically ill body – I have often had cause to ponder the meaning of them. At an important, lived level I have come to appreciate their wisdom. In accepting the realities of my body and coming to a rich and honest self-acceptance, I know only too well how the truth sets a person free. This freedom is not always easy; but it is real. To live in the truth is liberating. As we dwell deeper in the truth, we become freer and live a more complete and flourishing life.

Jesus goes further than my more popular reading of his words. He locates them, as ever, in relationship and community. To those who come to believe in him, he says if they abide in his word, they will truly be his disciples; as they dwell in the word, they will know the truth, and the truth will set them free. His followers respond by reminding him that as the descendants of Abraham and children of God's original covenant they have always been free; in effect, they have always lived in the truth. Jesus reminds them that birthright is not in and of itself a promise of abiding in the truth. It is only in relationship with the one who knows God the Father himself – the Son – that a sure and secure relationship with reality and truth is assured.

How might the idea that 'the truth will set you free' be an interesting and/or helpful way of understanding Elphaba's and Galinda's new awareness of each other?

How have you reflected on Jesus' famous words as applied to your own life and pilgrimage?

Can we be too individualistic in our reading of Jesus' words? How do you respond to Jesus' claim that true freedom is found in relationship with him?

LOOKING AHEAD ... ACTIVITIES TO CONSIDER THIS WEEK

While there is always space and value in our private prayers and devotions, the life to which we are called in prayer and worship is, ultimately, community-shaped. That is why Jesus reminds us that where two or three are gathered he is present. Even those who have the rare vocation to become a hermit or anchorite are not expected to be without human relationship, typically offering time and energy to pray and speak with those who seek their counsel. We are not Christians alone.

Given this truth, this week offers an opportunity not only to reflect on how each of us may better be united with others in worship and prayer, but also to take action. As a disabled person, one of the things which I become ever more aware of is how readily we exclude people from access to worship. This is not simply a matter of whether our church offers digital access to worship via Zoom or other sites; this is about attending to whether worship is disabled-accessible in any number of ways. What is worship like for wheelchair-users or those who might have sight or hearing impairments and so on? I have yet to attend a church which does not claim to be welcoming; sadly, this can so readily resolve into we are welcoming as long as you are 'like us' or like how we 'do things'. Consider undertaking a disability audit of your church space and worship to see where the challenges and opportunities are for your worship.

When I was a parish priest, one of the things with which I would regularly challenge myself and my PCC colleagues is with the question, 'Who is missing from our worship and fellowship?' Try asking it in your church. It reveals so much about the ways in which any fellowship has further to go in the work of growing into the likeness of Christ. In my last church, one of the things this question revealed was how middle-class and economically comfortable our fellowship was; yet we were set in a place where most people lacked that power. By attending to the absences in our fellowship it helped us reflect our community better, not least by challenging our assumptions about what an inclusive, welcoming church looked like. It was a slow work of transformation, but I remain convinced that God was asking us to undertake it. It was not an exercise in guilt tripping ourselves for our failures, but an attempt to embrace God's invitation to build a bigger table and a more spacious tent for all to come and be part of the community of love, justice and grace. This week, dare to ask yourself the question: who is missing from our worship and fellowship and how can we build a bigger, more welcoming table?

CLOSING PRAYER

Jesus Christ, Bread of Life,
you set a feast for your friends
and invite us to eat of your flesh
and drink your blood.
As we feast on you, shape us
into your Body and send us out
to be a feast of love and grace
in this world of need, in and through
your son our saviour Jesus Christ.
Amen.

REFLECTIONS

Use this space to record thoughts, responses and resolutions that have occurred to you during Week Three.

WEEK FOUR

'Popular' – The attractions and pitfalls of popularity and being liked

TO START YOU THINKING ...

We had been rehearsing for weeks, maybe even months. Our little, no-note school had never tried anything as ambitious as this in its history and frankly the budget was laughable. Staff and students had begged and borrowed wardrobe items and props. Charity shops had been scoured. One scene required swords, and someone had picked up some ornamental things from a tourist shop in Spain and sneaked them back in their luggage. The stage creaked in all the wrong places, and the lighting rig was not much more impressive than an array you might set up in your own home. Nonetheless, we had pulled it off: a staging of a Shakespeare history play, an idea of one of the more eccentric English teachers. And it had gone off pretty well: everyone had managed to memorise and deliver their sometimes vast speeches.

It was my first proper experience of 'treading the boards', but as first night ended, and we gathered at the front of the stage for the curtain call, my fifteen-year-old self experienced a drug unlike any other: applause. Applause from both adults and from peers and – given I had one of the main roles – I will never forget how I got my own spotlight moment and … Wow! People gave me a special cheer. I was hooked, and for years I volunteered for every play and opportunity to show off. When the applause was loud, I was happy; when it was absent I was depressed. I discovered, in ways I had barely appreciated before, that what I really wanted was approval, to receive this token of popularity and affirmation. I make no apology for describing applause as a drug. It is one of the most powerful on the planet. It is chased, whether literally or figuratively, by so many people, not just actors, but politicians and leaders of many varieties. Applause is a token of popularity and to be popular, especially when we are insecure or vulnerable, is not only appealing but can be a way to bolster our self-image.

Wicked skilfully explores the appeal of popularity and the ready buzz given when we receive the applause of the crowd. It captures the serial insecurities of youth, as well as the wider pressures and pleasures of being part of a community with defined boundaries, whether that be a school, university, religious community, church, club or an office, and so on. Both Galinda and Elphaba feel the pull and power of popularity. Fanned by charisma and charm, it can smooth our way in society and community and make us feel less insecure and isolated. It has its terrors too: what happens if I cease to be popular and the applause dies away? Who would I be, then? Equally, for some, the pressures of maintaining popularity and achieving celebrity can come with their own drawbacks. One can cease to be a private person and end up feeling like public property. Extreme popularity can distort one's sense of reality and self.

Jesus suggests that those who follow him should not expect to be popular. He suggests that the world will 'hate' those who follow the Way of God. He also says that those who will be persecuted for righteousness' sake will be blessed. The Way of Jesus is not a path to wild popularity. Why? Part of the answer lies in the challenge Jesus' path presents to our ordinary, conventional ways of going on. It critiques human self-centredness and selfishness, and challenges 'me, me, me' culture. The Way of Jesus also challenges greed and those practices which exploit the vulnerable or celebrate unbridled power and violence. Jesus invites us to prioritise Love above all else, and the evidence of history – and indeed of Jesus' own rejection by those he came to save – indicates that this is the toughest path of all. While the gospels suggest that there were times when Jesus himself was popular – after all, he was celebrated as he entered Jerusalem on Palm Sunday – ultimately he was abandoned to a criminal's death on a cross. When Pontius Pilate gave the crowd an opportunity to set Jesus or the criminal Barabbas free, the crowd chose Barabbas.

Wicked reminds us that there are many reasons why we might prefer to be popular. Certainly, there can be few of us who would actively wish to be disliked. Equally, many of us prefer to stay within the easy boundaries of what is popular among the crowd. It is safer to feel that you are going along with what either most people think is right or normal, or with what the most powerful or popular person thinks is right. No one wants to be turned against. So it's safer to keep our heads down and not rock the boat. It is better to claim the safety of the crowd or the noisiest, or the most intimidating people or person in the crowd.

The real challenge, however, in our Christian pilgrimage is to be unafraid to stand up for what is right, especially in times when it would be easier just to fit in. That is the cost of following Jesus: it has real-world implications that can scare the pants off us. For if the Way of Christ is about peace, mercy, justice and love, among other things, this is no mere set of beliefs that exist to make us feel better or comforted. It has implications for how we live, together and as individuals. At times this is likely to make us a little less popular than we might wish to be; it might even mean we are mocked or harassed by a crowd or by a powerful, popular figure who is intimidated by our bravery. Jesus reminds us that we should take up the Cross and follow him. Whatever else that path may lead to, and I believe it leads to life, it does not readily lead to more applause.

PRAYER

Living and Loving God,
when all the cheers and applause
this world offers fade away
you wait to meet us in your Son, Jesus Christ;
help us to take up the Cross and follow him;
fill us with your spirit of love
that we may have the courage to always
seek what is right and act for your justice
and mercy in this broken world.
Amen.

Read
John 15:18-25

Icebreaker
How do you imagine you might respond to being very popular with the public or being famous? Why?

WATCH

From 1.16.40 to the end of 'Popular' and Fiyero's encounter with Elphie outside the lecture hall (1.27.48).

In this very funny scene, we see Galinda and Elphaba as they become friends. Galinda challenges Elphaba to share a secret with her. Initially, Elphaba is reluctant, so Galinda shares a 'secret' of her own: she and Fiyero are going to get married (despite Fiyero not yet knowing!). Elphaba reluctantly shares her big secret: the reason her father hates her is because he blames her for Nessa's disability and for her mother's death. Galinda tells Elphaba that it cannot be her fault. She then has a brainwave: not only is she going to call Elphaba 'Elphie', but she is going to make her popular.

Galinda takes Elphaba through all the different strategies and techniques which promote popularity, most of which resolve into being more like Galinda. Elphaba is both mesmerised by Galinda and seems unsure whether she wants what she has to offer. We see Elphaba leave, a single rose in her hair, as Galinda sings, 'though you protest your disinterest, I know clandestinely, you're gonna grin and bear it, your newfound popularity'. Later, we see Elphaba practising her hair flick, a la Galinda, and Fiyero spots her and says she has been 'Galinda-fied'. He insists that she does not need to do that.

Think about

What do you make of the emergent relationship between Galinda and Elphaba?

What do you think of Galinda's 'recipe' for (female) popularity?

What must it be like for Elphaba to carry around the knowledge that her own father blames her for Nessa's disability and her mother's death?

To what extent do Elphaba and Galinda draw out something fresh or unexpected in their new friend?

Galinda suggests that life is not about 'aptitude' but about the 'way you're viewed'. Whether you like this claim or not, to what extent is it a smart and honest assessment of reality in an image-obsessed social media world?

GOING DEEPER

Read
2 Timothy 3:1-5

Paul's Second Letter to Timothy is one of those writings which has been subject to much critical reappraisal in recent centuries. Questions have been raised about its authorship. Was it written by Paul or by someone writing in his name, seeking to draw on his authority and teachings? Certainly, it is tonally and stylistically different from those letters, like the letter to the Romans or the Corinthian letters, we confidently attribute to Paul. Whatever, one's critical view, it continues to speak to Christians, especially those facing tough times and persecution.

This section from the Letter is one of Paul's classic 'be warned' lists. He reminds Timothy that in the final days before Christ's return there will be distressing times of trial. These trials might lead the faithful astray. Paul then outlines a gigantic and quite overwhelming list of those who, as heralds of distress, are to be avoided by those who wish to remain holy. The list includes those who love themselves, those who love money, and those who boast and are arrogant, to name just a few.

Why, in your view, does Paul group this list of people and behaviours as those to be avoided by the faithful of God?

Spend a few moments considering Paul's list of the 'naughty' in some detail. It is quite extensive! How do Galinda, Elphaba and the other characters from *Wicked* fare when placed against St Paul's list?

Could you or people you like and admire be included on that list? What are the implications of that? Should we be alarmed at how we readily fall short of the expectations of holiness?

WATCH

From the beginning of history class with Dr Dillamond (1 hr 27.49 mins) until the end of the encounter between Fiyero and Elphaba (1 hr 36.10 mins).

The history class gathers, and Dr Dillamond says this is his last day as a teacher, since animals have been banned from teaching. He is violently led away by the secret police and the University's head explains the class has a new teacher. Only Elphaba stands up and speaks out, frustrated that the others remain silent in the face of injustice. The new teacher wants to give a 'lesson in the future', sharing the concept of a 'cage' in which a small lion cub has been trapped. Again, only Elphaba speaks up against it. In her anger she performs magic which sends everyone except for her, Fiyero and the lion cub to sleep. Fiyero leaps into action, and they escape with the cub into the forest. Madame Morrible sees the students asleep and writes to the Wizard of Oz about Elphaba's abilities.

Before setting the cub free, Elphaba and Fiyero speak. Fiyero asks why Elphaba is always causing commotions, and she explains that she is a commotion. She asks if he thinks she should just keep her mouth shut. This descends into a tiff in which Fiyero struggles to be heard. They touch hands and there is is a deep crackle of attraction between them. Fiyero runs off with the cub saying he must get it to safety. As he runs off Elphaba calls out his name tenderly.

Think about

Elphaba risks unpopularity and censure by speaking out for justice for the animals. The rest of the class stays silent. What is it that keeps them silent? Can it sometimes be wiser to remain silent in the short term rather than speak out?

Elphaba tells Fiyero that she knows life would be easier for her if she cared less about justice and rights. To what extent do you think she is right to care so much? What would be lost if she was like most people?

What stops Elphaba and Fiyero from acting on their attraction to one another? What would be placed at risk if they were honest about how they feel?

GOING DEEPER

Read
Ecclesiastes 3:1-8

This justly famous passage – like the book of Ecclesiastes itself – is a summation of wisdom drawn from a lifetime. Unlike some of the books of the Bible, it bears the hallmark of the influence of Greek philosophical thought on Jewish thinking. There is a worldly-wise desire to comprehend the puzzling nature of an often scary and unstable world and pass on life lessons. Perhaps that is why it remains popular at funerals: it provides a view of life drawn from a summation of experience.

The fundamental thrust of the passage is that there is a time and a season for everything on earth: a time for birth and a time for death, a time to break down and a time to build up, among many other things. There are phrases in this passage I find almost unutterably moving like 'a time to mourn and a time to dance' or 'a time to tear, and a time to sew'. Others – like a time to kill, and a time to heal or a time for war and a time for peace – have troubled me. When I was a young pacifist vegetarian,[8] I could not accept that there is a time to kill. Now, that I am older I have come to a richer, subtler understanding of these words. Ultimately, the challenge of this passage is to wrestle with when something is in season or out of season; when is the time to act or speak or to remain silent, for example. This discernment is something I think we need to do both as individuals and as communities.

The passage suggests that there is a time to speak and a time to keep silent. How might that inform Elphaba's behaviour in response to the abduction of Dr Dillamond?

In our own society and world, there are many occasions when we have to discern what it is appropriate to speak out about. What skills and principles do you use to help you discern?

While there may be a time and a season for everything, can that claim be used as an alibi or excuse not to address what is really going on? (For example, Fiyero clearly finds Elphaba deeply attractive but could argue that 'now is not the right time to express it' or the students at Shiz might say that while what is happening to the animals is unjust, it would be 'better to wait for the right time before protesting against it.')

---

[8] Truth is, I'm neither of those things now.

WATCH

From Elphaba calling out Fiyero's name (1 hr 36.10 mins) up to the end of 'I'm Not That Girl' (1.39.36 mins).

In this song, Elphaba acknowledges her love for Fiyero whilst recognising that she cannot 'compete' with what Galinda offers. She is not the girl Fiyero has chosen. Elphaba tries to remind herself not to lose sight of who she is and suggests that wishing for something other than reality 'only wounds the heart'; as much as we might have a longing to go to the land of 'what-might-have-been' it does not soften the ache when reality sets back in.

She compares herself unfavourably with Galinda. As we look on with Elphaba, we see Galinda greet Fiyero. Fiyero clearly looks back behind him; he is still thinking about Elphaba but she is unable to recognise this gesture for what it is. She concludes that she is not born for the 'rose and pearl' and therefore she is not the girl Fiyero wants to be with.

Think about
Elphaba suggests that 'wishing only wounds the heart'. How true is that? What is the place of dreams and wishes in a flourishing life?

Elphaba is clearly a hugely caring, talented and – now – accepted and popular student. Nonetheless, she cannot seem to see herself as attractive. Why, in your view, is that?

Why do we humans so often struggle to see ourselves as clearly and honestly as we would like?

GOING DEEPER

Read
1 Corinthians 13

I was in two minds as to whether to suggest this passage for this 'going deeper' section. It is almost too famous. I think of it as one of the 'proof texts' of the Bible – a passage so strong and beautiful and hope-filled that it reveals the inescapable truth of the Bible. It is embedded deeply in the wider culture as one of the passages that is known by those who are not committed Christians. It has been used at countless weddings and increasingly also at funerals.

So why use it in this context? Well, I am mesmerised by those words of Paul which remind us that now – in this life, from our perspective – we know only in part; we are limited and contingent creatures. As he reminds us, when we are children we are limited to childish things; when we become adults we trust we are able to put away childish ways. Nonetheless, in this life we 'see through a mirror dimly'; we cannot hope to have a full and complete grasp on life. Our hope for fullest understanding lies in the Lord: when we come to the completeness of creation, the fulness of our meeting with God in Jesus Christ, we will 'see face to face'.

I take huge comfort from Paul's words. It is a reminder that we do not need to be afraid of our mortal limitations and provides a warm, realistic assessment of why, so often, we struggle to judge ourselves or others as clearly as we might. It is immensely helpful, I think, in helping us both to be kind to ourselves and others but also draws us back to the flowing heart of creation: that without love, each of us is nothing. For love never ends; and though faith, hope and love abide, the greatest of these is love. It is the heartbeat and the lifeblood of the universe.

How does Paul's suggestion that we see 'through a mirror dimly' help us understand why Elphaba (and indeed ourselves) fail to see ourselves and others clearly?

Paul prioritises love above all else. Why? And what do you think he means by 'love'?

What does the word 'love' mean for you? To what extent are we inclined to place the kind of romantic love Elphaba and Fiyero feel above other kinds of love? Why?

LOOKING AHEAD ... ACTIVITIES TO CONSIDER THIS WEEK

In its sub-plot concerning Dr Dillamond and the treatment of the animals, *Wicked* explores what happens when a society creates scapegoats as a means to bring it together; it is a political strategy as old as time which continues to be deployed by 'populist' and extremist politicians in our own day. By exploiting fear for propaganda opportunities, groups and individuals can end up – through no fault of their own – not only unpopular but treated as a threat.

In light of the above, consider spending some time this week exploring who are the equivalents (or near equivalents) of Oz's animals in our own world and society. Another way of exploring this is to ask, 'Who are the people and the groups who are on God of Justice's heart?' I imagine there will be a range of responses to that question, though I would be amazed if you do not have a list.

The challenge then is to consider how one might add one's voice – or better, the voice of your Church – to support the groups/individuals on your list. One route can be financial: there are almost always charitable opportunities to support groups who are penalised or excluded. Another is advocacy. Could you work with your church leadership on how your church might become more effective advocates, perhaps by inviting a speaker or organisation to give a talk at your church or synod? If you are more politically engaged with your church's national structures what are the ways you can get advocacy and justice onto the agenda?

As ever, begin and end in prayer. When we ask ourselves a question like, 'Who are the people and the groups who are on God's heart?' we are really asking, 'Who should be on our hearts, God?' Quite naturally it follows on from this to ask God to lead us into action which unites our hearts with his. If we do this, we will not go far wrong; we shall draw closer to the likeness of Christ.

CLOSING PRAYER

O God of Grace and Welcome,
lead us always into the ways of love
shown forth in your son Jesus Christ;
grant to us wisdom and discernment
and the courage to rejoice
in the rich diversity of the peoples
of your good earth.
Amen.

REFLECTIONS

Use this space to record thoughts, responses and resolutions that have occurred to you during Week Four.

WEEK FIVE

'Defying Gravity' – The joy and cost of seeing the world more clearly and living life authentically

TO START YOU THINKING ...

Who am I? This or the other?
Am I one person today and tomorrow another?
Am I both at once? A hypocrite before others,
And before myself a contemptibly woebegone
   weakling?
Or is something within me still like a beaten army,
Fleeing in disorder from victory already achieved?
Who am I? They mock me, these lonely questions
   of mine.
Whoever I am, Thou knowest, O God, I am Thine![9]

Dietrich Bonhoeffer's famous poem of doubt and faith, written during his imprisonment in Tegel Prison, has become a classic text in spiritual direction. It examines Bonhoeffer's feelings of disconnect between his inner narrative (insecure, lacking in faith, uncertain either of his own presence or that of God) and the public behaviour he performs in front of others (bold, encouraging, lovingly present to both his fellow prisoners and his Nazi prison guards).

This poem was one of the very first things given to me by my first spiritual director after I came to faith in my mid-twenties. He was alert, I think, to how Bonhoeffer's anxieties about himself and God found an analogue in my own journey both as a new Christian and as a trans woman. As a Christian I was concerned with discerning the ways in which my 'inner' sense of faith

[9] Dietrich Bonhoeffer, *Letters and Papers from Prison* (first published 1951).

and God might come alive in prayer, worship, and social commitment. As a trans woman, who had transitioned three years before, I was still exploring what living as a woman – as a day to day lived reality that was often called into question by verbal abuse and misgendering, etc. – meant in terms of my inner life.

In this final session of this Lent course, *Wicked* shows us what can happen when a person – in this case Elphaba – brings together her inner sense of self with public action in the face of condemnation. In her magnificent tour de force, 'Defying Gravity', Elphaba finally embraces what she wants – to be herself without the need for approval from or reference to the Wizard and the rest of society – and begins to put this into action. It involves rejection of a safe place with the Wizard and places her friendship with the much more conformist Glinda in jeopardy. As she follows her conscience she is scapegoated as dangerous and evil.

It is, perhaps, unsurprising that Elphaba's Defying Gravity moment would be something of a rallying cry for many who either long to step outside of stifling convention or find they must do so because they do not fit societal conventions. I think part of the reason I love this song and the character of Elphaba is because I know what it is not to fit in. While I hold all sorts of privilege in our society – most significantly, being white – I know what it is to be categorised as an 'oddity' and an 'outsider'. That is simply how it is when you are disabled, trans, neurodiverse, a woman, and chronically ill (among other things) in a society like ours. Like Elphaba, I know what it is to step outside of convention and take the risk of claiming space and personal power. I know the cost of stepping outside convention. As a trans woman I have had to resist, day after day, countless voices who say that what I feel and desire is impossible.

Elphaba discovers that her vocation is to be her true self. In that sense, she is on a spiritual quest. One does not need to be like Elphaba or like me to know the power and reality of that quest. To be a Christian is, in many ways, to be concerned with the call to 'be one's true self.' That call is a process of growing into the likeness of Christ and it is shaped around prayer, action, and discernment, grounded in scripture and self-examination.

Bonhoeffer's question 'Who am I?' matters because 'Who I am or see myself to be' will be crucial in revealing how I see God and vice versa. That is, one's images of oneself is a guide to one's images of God and vice versa. The Christian faith reminds us that this vocation to become our true selves is a lifetime's work. Thomas Merton famously suggests each of us can give no greater glory to God than being ourselves – our true selves.[10] A tree, for example, gives glory to God by being a tree. However, for the tree that is not difficult because it cannot be other than its essential 'tree-ness'. For humans, however, it is terribly complicated: we have so many possibilities and paths before us. We are marked by a combination of sin and free will. We can and often do choose to be other than our true selves. Thus, Merton argues, the only way any of us can know and be truly ourselves, is to know ourselves in God. For only God sees the picture clearly. Only God holds me in my completeness. On this account, a journey into self, then, is a journey into God.

As this course draws to a close, this is quite a thought for any of us to consider. There is huge power in Elphaba's moment when she defies gravity and breaks free. The same is true for any one of us who makes necessary and important steps to break free from an oppressive or repressive situation or way of life; there is great power in being oneself. At the same time, Merton and other spiritual masters remind us that our truest self

---

[10] Merton, T. (1962), *Seeds of Contemplation*, London, Burns & Oates.

and deepest liberation is found in relationship with the living God. Elphaba might sing, 'If I'm flying solo at least I'm flying free', but there is – in the Christian story – a deeper challenge to discover our true freedom in the company of the living God and through that, solidarity with the people of his pasture.

PRAYER

O God of Liberation,
in you is true life and freedom
and the promise of salvation;
help us to walk the road to freedom
with and in your son our saviour Jesus
Christ. Be with us when we seek to break
out of patterns of violence and abuse
stir your people to follow the paths of justice
and look on us in mercy when we lose our way.
Amen.

Read
Matthew 16:24-26

Icebreaker
How do you respond to the idea that each of us is called to live our true selves? What steps have you taken to grow into that true self?

WATCH

From: Madame Morrible calling out Elphaba's name (1.39.38) up to the end of 'One Short Day' (1.54.02).

Elphaba receives an invite from the Wizard of Oz to meet him in the Emerald City. She is nervous about the visit and Galinda does her best to be glad for her. A train arrives to take Elphaba away, and Galinda, without Fiyero, comes to say goodbye. Galinda is worried about him. He has changed since the arrest of Dr Dillamond. When he arrives to say goodbye, he begins to speak about the lion cub and Dr Dillamond and almost professes his love for Elphaba.

Galinda decides to turn the focus back onto herself by announcing – as an act of solidarity with Dr Dillamond – that she is changing her name to 'Glinda'. Glinda almost immediately regrets the decision, but Elphaba tells her it does not matter as everyone loves her. For the first time, Glinda feels vulnerable: she wants Fiyero but is, half-consciously, aware that he does not want her. As the students cheer, Elphaba leaves. Glinda gives her a guide to the Emerald City in which she has written 'I hope you get what your heart desires'. Elphaba realises she wants Glinda to come, and they go to the Emerald City. As they travel around, they are filled with awe and great excitement.

They watch a show which tells the 'absolutely factual story' of the Wizard of Oz.[11] It explains that long ago, the

---

[11] The two performers are played by Idina Menzel and Kristin Chenoweth, who originated the roles of Elphaba and Glinda on Broadway in 2003.

Magical Wise Ones wrote down their knowledge in a secret language in the Book of Grimmerie. Before their demise, the Wise Ones' prophesy that in Oz's darkest hour a person will arise who can read the Grimmerie and save Oz. One day, a man arrives in a balloon and, as the story has it, he can read the book and is proclaimed the 'Wizard of Oz'. As Elphaba and Glinda prepare to meet him, they declare their friendship: Elphaba says they are good friends, and Glinda says they are best friends.

Think about
For the first time, Glinda begins to realise that she is not so different from others, despite Elphaba telling her she is loved by everyone. Have you ever had to face a reality about yourself that is uncomfortable or challenging and how did you respond?

Why in your view does Elphaba bring Glinda along to the Emerald City?

Glinda and Elphaba watch a show in the Emerald City that claims to be the 'absolutely factual story' of Oz. What reasons might there be for us to be suspicious of that claim?

What do you make of Elphaba and Glinda's different understandings of their friendship?

GOING DEEPER

Read
John 15:12-17

Our society adores friendship. Social media has taken the word and run with it; when I was still on the platform, I revelled in the number of Facebook 'friends' I had, many of whom I'd never actually met physically but with whom I regularly interacted. Such connections helped me curate an image of myself as popular and influential. In her recent book, *Friendaholic*, Elizabeth Day suggests that in a world of often fleeting romantic and sexual relationships, friendship – especially being able to say one has friends that go back to childhood – can offer a psychological life jacket, most particularly for women, in a fast-moving, unstable world. For some, and especially some of my LGBT+ friends whose families have rejected them, friendship becomes a way of developing a found family of significant, stable, and supportive relationships.

In this passage, Jesus suggests that friendship is one of the fundamentals of divine love. On the night before he died, as he prepares for betrayal, he gives to his closest disciples a new commandment: that they love one another as he has loved them. Tellingly, Jesus unpacks this commandment through friendship rather than through ideas of family or work or power obligations. He says that the greatest love is shown in the willingness to lay down one's life for one's friends. He calls his disciples his friends. As Christ faces his end, he prioritises friendship; he resets the relationship between God and humanity from master/servant to friend amongst friends.

When placed in the light of Jesus' words, how robust do you think Elphaba and Glinda's friendship is?

Can friendship truly be the kind of load-bearing, fundamental relationship Jesus suggests it is?

Friendship is not simply about sharing pleasures and fascinations in common, but about what abides in times of trial and trouble. To what extent do you agree or disagree?

In Jesus' famous speech when he calls his disciples 'friends,' he says, 'You are my friends if you do what I command.' What do you make of Jesus' statement?

WATCH

From the fireworks exploding (1.54.00) up to where Elphaba runs away from the Wizard (2.11.55).

Elphaba and Glinda enter the Wizard's palace and are led by Chistery past many armed monkeys into the presence of the Wizard. They are greeted by a giant face with glowing eyes and Elphaba wants to run away. When the face speaks it says it is Oz the Great and Terrible. However, as soon as Elphaba introduces herself the voice becomes human and the face stops moving. Elphaba and Glinda discover that Oz is actually a man. He is excited to meet Elphaba but practically ignores Glinda.

The Wizard shares his vision of the Oz of Tomorrow in model form. He plans to build a road that will give people 'direction'; by following the road Ozians will always find their way to the Wizard. He shows Elphaba a model figure he has made of her. It is green. The model helps Elphaba realise that her heart's desire is no longer to be degreenified but for the Wizard to help the animals. He agrees that something needs to be done.

He claims that what he loves best is making people happy and sings 'A Sentimental Man' about how he had always longed to be a father and treat everyone in Oz like a son or daughter. He disappears behind a curtain and charms Elphaba and Glinda with a magic show. Madame Morrible arrives and Elphaba is shown the Grimmerie. Both the Wizard and Morrible hint that Elphaba might not be able to cast a spell from it, perhaps to goad her, but Elphaba wants to prove herself.

The book opens immediately for Elphaba, to the shock of the others. The Wizard suggests that Chistery would like wings. Elphaba wants to help and the Grimmerie magically opens to a specific page. Elphaba discovers that she can read the lost language with fluency. As she says the spell, in agony Chistery grows wings. Elphaba is horrified. Everyone is shocked and in awe. Elphaba wants to reverse the spell. To her horror, all the other monkeys have grown wings too.

The Wizard and Morrible are thrilled and say that the monkeys will make perfect spies. Elphaba is shocked and disgusted. The Wizard then reveals he wants scouts to report 'seditious animal activity'. We discover that the Wizard is the person who is responsible for the oppression of the animals. Glinda tries to justify his behaviour by explaining that she is sure he has a good reason. Morrible says they are doing it to keep all of Oz safe. The Wizard, however, offers his own justification: he claims that when he arrived in Oz, he found discontent and he is doing what he had learned back home - that the best way to bring folks together is to give them a 'real good enemy'.

Elphaba realises that the Wizard has no magical power: he cannot make spies himself and he cannot read the Grimmerie. He has no real power, so he needs Elphaba to maintain the trappings of power. The Wizard tries to use Glinda to get her to listen to him and Morrible. She does her best. Elphaba refuses the offer to be with him and runs off with the Grimmerie.

Think about
Why does the Wizard use fire and noise and a mask to greet people who come into his presence? He says he likes to come across as charming and sentimental, but what are the clues that he might be a little sinister?

Glinda seems very keen to please the Wizard and explain/justify his actions. Why?

In this sequence, we see that the Wizard is a trickster who wants control and Elphaba sees him (and Morrible) clearly for the first time. Have you ever had such an epiphany or realisation? If you feel able to do so, speak a little about what that was like.

In our own world, what examples can you think of when those who want power or to maintain power give people a 'real, good enemy' to hate? How can we counteract such situations?

GOING DEEPER

Read
Ephesians 4:25-32

The Letter to the Ephesians is about unity and holiness. It offers proposals for the people of God to live well together and how they can struggle against all that which can draw them away from God. In the closing section of chapter four, Paul requests that the Christians at Ephesus put away falsehood and speak truth to one another, 'for we are members of one another'. Anger is permitted, he says, as long as that does not tumble over into sin. The sun should not be allowed to go down on anger. 'Evil talk' must not be permitted to be spoken but only what is useful for building up and for the sharing of grace. For Paul, kindness, tender-heartedness, and forgiveness should, ultimately, be the marker of a community shaped by God's forgiveness.

When Elphaba meets the Wizard, does she put away falsehood and speak truth? Paul suggests that Christians should do this because 'we are members of one another'. Can that be said to apply to in the 'relationship' between the Wizard and Elphaba?

Elphaba is understandably angry with the Wizard and Madame Morrible and their trickery and lies. Yet St Paul says, 'The sun should not be allowed to go down on your anger.' What does this phrase mean? What are the dangers and risks of anger?

Can we treat the falsehoods and lies of the Wizard and Morrible as 'evil talk'? To what extent does Glinda, in her need to stay on side with them, risk falling into 'evil talk'?

St Paul emphasises the importance of using what we say to 'build up'; equally, kindness and tender-heartedness are markers of Christian community. Is there an argument to say that Elphaba would have been wiser or better off by adopting this approach? Is it the approach Glinda adopts?

WATCH

From: Elphaba running away (2.11.55) up to the 'To Be Continued' Credits (2.30.50)

As Elphaba runs off, Madame Morrible threatens Glinda, saying, 'If you want to do yourself some good, get her back.' Glinda chases after Elphaba. Morrible also threatens the monkeys and sets them to capture Elphaba. The Wizard commissions the guards to capture the 'fugitive' too.

Elphaba and Glinda run off into the Wizard's balloon chamber, closely followed by the guards. They inflate the balloon and fight off the guards. The guards close the roof and prevent their escape and Elphaba uses a broom to bar the door of the room into which they have escaped. Glinda reasons with Elphaba again asking her to let the Wizard explain his behaviour. Elphaba refuses. Glinda gets angry with her, saying this situation is bigger than both of them and asking why she could not have stayed calm for once instead of flying off the handle. Angrily she says she hopes Elphaba is happy, having destroyed her dreams. Elphaba retorts by angrily saying she hopes Glinda is happy too, grovelling in submission to feed her own ambition.

Morrible warns the citizens of Oz about Elphaba: she is an evil enemy who is a liar and a thief, who has mutilated monkeys. She claims that Elphaba's green skin is but an 'outward manifestation of her twisted nature'. Glinda realises that this propaganda will be irresistible and tells Elphaba not to be afraid. She replies that it is the Wizard who should be afraid of her.

Glinda again tries to make peace and asks Elphaba to say sorry to the Wizard and she can still have all she ever wanted. Elphaba says she knows this, but has realised she does not and cannot want it anymore. She has changed. She realises she has woken up and will not play by another person's rules anymore. She wants to try defying gravity. Glinda warns her that she is having delusions of grandeur. As the guards close in, Elphaba tries the 'wing-growing' spell again, but instead of being able to fly she enchants a broom, which flies up to her.

Elphaba offers Glinda a chance to escape with her, telling her to think of what they could do together. They picture themselves together as 'unlimited', the greatest team there has ever been. They rejoice together in the realisation. However, Glinda finds she cannot leave. It is a moment of deep friendship and deep loss, as they realise their difference. Glinda dresses Elphaba in a black cloak and they wish each other happiness and fulfilment, and they part as friends.

Glinda is grabbed by the guards as Elphaba flies off. Initially, Elphaba falls towards the earth in distress, as she remembers her childhood and the awful way she was treated by her father and the local children. She then has a vision of herself as a child and realises it is time to embrace both who she was and has become. Child and adult Elphaba reach out for each other and, confident at last, the broom flies into Elphaba's hand. As Elphaba flies free and alone, Madame Morrible realises she can use Glinda for her own unpleasant purposes. We see Fiyero leaving Shiz in light of the news he has heard about Elphaba. We see Elphaba soar as the Wizard looks on in fear.

Think about

What is it about Glinda that means she acts on behalf of the Wizard and Madame Morrible? Her need for approval and popularity, her fear, her weakness, or what?

What do you make of Madame Morrible in this sequence? Does her behaviour (and that of the Wizard) find echoes in the behaviour of some of the political leaders in our own world?

Elphaba says she has 'woken up' (is she 'woke'?) and will no longer play by someone else's rules. Yet she is scapegoated as evil and monstrous. Who could be the equivalents of the 'wicked witch' in our world?

Elphaba says that if she is flying solo at least she is flying free. What do you make of that statement? Do you agree or disagree? Why?

Elphaba and Glinda realise that together they would be an unlimited team. What qualities do each have would that make that true? What stops them from teaming up?

Are you surprised that they are able to part as friends? Why can they do this?

GOING DEEPER

Read
Luke 4:16-30

Quite often this passage is known as the 'Nazareth Manifesto' because it sets out Jesus' priorities for his ministry. After his baptism and forty days in the Wilderness, he returns to his home village of Nazareth. His reading from Isaiah is the proclamation not only of God's priorities, but himself as the fulfilment of them. Jesus has been anointed to bring good news to the poor, to proclaim release to the captives, recovery of sight to the blind, to let the oppressed go free, and to proclaim the year of the Lord's favour. Initially he is treated well by his old village: the people speak well of him and with amazement. Can this be the son of the carpenter?

Yet, Jesus reads the people of his village with clear eyes: what they would like is for a taste of the Spirit-filled teaching he displayed in Capernaum. Indeed, he says, 'Truly I tell you, no prophet is accepted in the prophet's hometown.' He shares the story of Elijah who, during the time of a great famine, was not sent to Israel's widows but to the widow at Zarephath in Sidon; he also speaks of Elisha's time when there were also many lepers in Israel, but none were cleansed except Naaman the Syrian. This enrages the congregation in the synagogue, and they drive Jesus out of town, and lead him to the brow of the hill, so that they might hurl him off the cliff. But he passes through the midst of them and goes on his way.

Jesus and Elphaba are quite different figures; nonetheless, they can both be divisive. What is it about each of them that means they can enrage others?

Why do we often get excited about having a hometown hero or star with whom we can claim a connection and feel proud? Do you have any examples from where you grew up or have lived?

What is the deep message Jesus is trying to communicate to the people of Nazareth about the Gospel? Why is he seemingly so rude to them?

'The truth shall set you free ...' However, it would also seem that for both Jesus and Elphaba it is costly too. What is it about the truth that can bring great costs? (And why are they worth bearing?)

LOOKING AHEAD ... ACTIVITIES TO CONSIDER THIS WEEK

This final week has explored themes of uncovering the truth and what it means to live authentically, as well as the ugly things the powerful will do to keep their position and grow in power. Despite *Wicked* being set in a world far from that of Jesus, these themes surely chime extraordinarily well with the world-changing events of Holy Week and Easter.

As such, as this course draws to a close and we look towards the events of Holy Week and Easter, we have a real opportunity to undertake some deep self-examination, asking ourselves what is getting in the way of a truer, more authentic pilgrimage with Jesus Christ. I have always been moved by the Wild Goose Worship Group's song, 'Travelling the Road to Freedom', often sung on Palm Sunday and during Holy Week. I invite you to take some time to look it up and meditate on the lyrics.[12] Even better, see if you can use it in worship and ask God to help you and your community to travel the costly road to freedom with Jesus.

For those who are strongly drawn to social action, consider how you might support organisations and charities like Amnesty International and Liberty, which

---

[12] This a beautiful free version of the song, including lyrics: https://thecathedral.bandcamp.com/track/travelling-the-road-to-freedom-john-l-bell-and-graham-maule. It is likely that other versions can be found on YouTube too,

are committed to promoting freedom from oppression and repression. While it is challenging to negotiate the swamp of fake news and so-called 'alternative facts' these organisations seek to ensure that the human rights of all people, especially the most marginalised and othered, are respected. Equally, organisations like Christian Aid, Tearfund, and CAFOD, among many others, pursue the holy ways of justice in deeply practical and pragmatic ways on the international stage.

Finally, the events of Holy Week and Easter present an opportunity above all others to recommit ourselves to Jesus Christ. I can think of no greater and more awesome calling than to walk with Jesus through those events leading up to and including his crucifixion and resurrection. They are not only moving, but life changing. So if you are unable to offer anything else this year, please find a way to participate in Holy Week; to pray, meditate and engage in the life, death, and resurrection of the one who is the very heart of love and the redeemer of all.

REFLECTIONS

Use this space to record thoughts, responses and resolutions that have occurred to you during Week Five.

POSTSCRIPT

I hope this course has both encouraged and challenged you. Most of all, I hope it has helped you step deeper into your relationship with Jesus Christ and become ever more alert to how God and God's work can be discerned in film and culture. If you have stayed with the course up to this point, I trust that – even if you were initially suspicious – you have discovered that the story of witches in the land of Oz reveals fresh horizons to this life of Christ to which we are called.

Courses like this can spark a hunger for further opportunities to meet and discuss the spiritual horizons of films. If this has been the case for your group, there are now many courses and study guides available. The publisher of this one, Darton, Longman and Todd, has many options. Do check out their website and back catalogue. If you have enjoyed this course, I guarantee you will find others suitable not only during Lent but throughout the year.

I also hope this book inspires you to engage with cinema and other forms of visual culture with fresh eyes. While I would be cautious about saying that every film or TV show is 'about God', God is there waiting in the most surprising places. Dare to take a look. God is so vibrantly alive in this world, it would be bizarre if our visual culture had managed to excise him. So, from time to time, take a risk and dare to watch films with a fresh eye. God, in my experience, has usually got there before us.